Autism & PDD ™
Abstract Concepts

#49938523

Linda Mulstay-Muratore

Skill Area:	Abstract language concepts
Ages:	5 through 9
Grades:	K through 4

LinguiSystems ®

LinguiSystems, Inc.
3100 4th Avenue
East Moline, IL 61244-9700
1-800-PRO IDEA
1-800-776-4332

FAX: 1-800-577-4555
E-mail: service@linguisystems.com
Web: www.linguisystems.com
TDD: 1-800-933-8331
(for those with hearing impairments)

Printed in the U.S.A.

ISBN 0-7606-0459-2

About the Author

Linda Mulstay-Muratore, M.A., CCC-SLP, has worked as a speech-language pathologist in private practice since her graduation in 1996 from St. John's University in New York. She gained her experience with children with PDD/autism and Applied Behavior Analysis (ABA) while in college working with families in home based educational ABA programs. Linda now does both consulting and direct therapy for children in early intervention and preschool, writing programs for and working in conjunction with teams of special educators.

Autism & PDD: Abstract Concepts, Level 2 is Linda's second publication with LinguiSystems. She is also the author of *Autism & PDD: Abstract Concepts, Level 1.*

Dedication

For my husband, Tom, who is forever encouraging and supportive: thank you for your unconditional love and making every day full of laughter!

Cover design & illustrations by Michael Paustian
Page layout by Denise L. Kelly

Table of Contents

# Introduction

Autism & PDD: Abstract Concepts, Level 2 was created for children aged five through nine who understand basic *Wh* questions, but have had difficulty advancing to comprehending more challenging linguistic and cognitive concepts. Specifically, children with a diagnosis of autism or pervasive developmental disorder (PDD) often have strong visual and concrete thinking skills, but lack the ability to think abstractly or out of a specific context. *Autism & PDD: Abstract Concepts, Level 2* uses simple, uncluttered illustrations as visual prompts and cues to help such children bridge the gap between concrete and abstract language.

Although some children can learn the correct response to these questions simply through rote memorization in discrete trials, allowing a child to visualize the concept provides the opportunity to actually understand the questions and the logic behind the responses. As the child expands his facility to answer the questions in this book, fade the visual prompts until the child generalizes his knowledge to everyday situations.

Instruction Guidelines

- Children should be able to understand and answer simple *who, what,* and *where* questions before beginning this material.

- If you are using the pictures in discrete trials, you may want to copy and laminate each picture for quick access. Allow the child to color the pictures as instructed with dry-erase markers so the pictures can be used again.

- Read the instructions at the beginning of each section before starting.

- Accept responses as correct if they are appropriate and logical. Examples of logical answers are listed in the Answer Key, pages 191-196.

- Model correct grammar and syntax when necessary.

- Begin training with one target question form at a time. Once the child masters more than one target question form, intermix these question forms in random order without using picture cues. The child demonstrates mastery of these forms by answering similar questions appropriately and logically intermittently throughout your sessions and in natural contexts.

- When applicable, suggested Short Term Objectives (STOs) in data collection for discrete trial training using this book are as follows:

STO 1: Full modeled prompt with pictures in view

Present the picture and read the question to the child. Provide a verbal model and have the child repeat it. Advance to STO 2 when the child is able to repeat a correct response with 90% accuracy over 2-3 consecutive days.

STO 2: Independent responses with pictures in view

Allow the child time to respond independently. If the child correctly responds independently with 90% accuracy over 2-3 consecutive days, move on to STO 3.

STO 3: Independent responses, pictures not in view

Allow the child time to respond appropriately. If the child responds appropriately with 90% accuracy over 2-3 consecutive days, move on to STO 4.

STO 4: Independent responses, pictures not in view, with question forms in random order

Intermix the target question form with other question forms the child has already mastered. Allow the child time to respond appropriately. Mastery of a question form is achieved when the child answers the target question form appropriately when asked in random order with other question forms, with 90% accuracy over 2-3 consecutive days.

I enjoyed creating these functional language training materials for my students, especially those with autism or PDD. I hope you find them helpful with your students as well.

Linda

Before beginning this section, review the feelings *disappointed, embarrassed, frustrated, proud, surprised,* and *nervous* with the child. Draw pictures of faces with various expressions. Name one of these expressions and have the child identify the feeling by pointing to the correct picture. Have the child make his own faces to reflect these emotions while looking in the mirror.

Directions

1. Photocopy each picture before presenting it to the child.

2. Have the child look at the picture. Read the question at the top of the page and allow the child time to think about and formulate a correct response.

3. Ask the child to draw in the character's mouth after giving a correct response. If the child is unable to draw the mouth, use hand-over-hand guidance to help the child complete the picture. If the child does not provide a correct response, model the appropriate response and repeat the question. In this case, drawing in the mouth serves as a visual prompt.

Example

Stimulus (page 8) ⟶

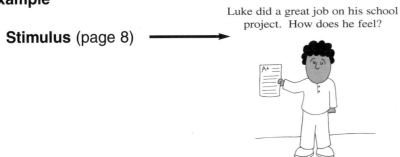

Luke did a great job on his school project. How does he feel?

Appropriate Responses

Beginner	**Intermediate**	**Advanced**
⬇	⬇	⬇
Single-Word Response	Multiple-Word Response	Complex Utterance
"Proud."	"Boy proud."	"The boy is proud."

Other Suggestions

• Have the child act out the pictured situation and demonstrate an appropriate response in symbolic play.

• Continue to explore other feelings, such as *excited, jealous,* and *anxious.*

Luke did a great job on his school project. How does he feel?

Alex is trying hard to build a model airplane, but it's not staying together. How does he feel?

Jenna scored the most runs in a game. How does she feel?

Jeremy is trying hard to do his homework,
but he just can't do it. How does he feel?

Michael really wants to go swimming, but his mom said it's too cold. How does he feel?

Devin is going to a new school. He doesn't know anybody. How does he feel?

Erin is telling her dog to sit, but he won't listen.
How does she feel?

Seth tripped down the stairs and everyone was looking.
How does he feel?

Tyler's grandmother kissed him in front of all his friends.
How does he feel?

Justin really wants to play outside with his friends, but he has to do his homework. How does he feel?

Brian is dancing and everyone is laughing at him.
How does he feel?

Mariah walked into her house and all of her friends were hiding. They yelled, "Happy Birthday!" How does she feel?

Zachary has to take a big test. He doesn't know
how he will do. How does he feel?

Colin didn't think he would like spinach, but he tried it and he liked it. How does he feel?

How often have you looked over at a crying, laughing, or juice-soaked child and asked, "What happened?" The ability to provide simple responses to this question help to explain playground disagreements or accidents at home, as well as to prevent future frustration, tantrums, or verbal outbursts.

Directions

1. Photocopy each picture before presenting it to the child.

2. Have the child look at the picture. Read the question "What happened?" Allow the child time to think about and formulate a response. If the child responds correctly, have the child color in the part of the picture that is significant to the answer. For example, if a picture shows a girl writing on a boy's cast on his arm, have the child color the boy's cast. This coloring may serve as a reinforcer. If the child does not respond correctly, model the correct response and repeat the question. Color the part of the picture that is significant to the response. In this case, the coloring may serve as a prompt.

Example

Stimulus (page 23) ──────▶

What happened?

Appropriate Responses

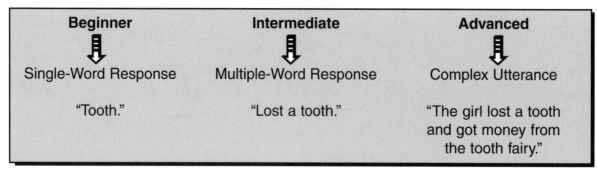

Beginner	Intermediate	Advanced
⬇	⬇	⬇
Single-Word Response	Multiple-Word Response	Complex Utterance
"Tooth."	"Lost a tooth."	"The girl lost a tooth and got money from the tooth fairy."

Other Suggestions

• Act out simple cause/effect situations. For example, "accidentally" step in a puddle or write on your hand. Have the child explain what happened.

• Have the child "tattle" or tell on you to his or her parent or sibling for behaving silly, "breaking" something, etc., during your session.

What happened?

What happened?

What happened?

What happened?

What happened?

What happened?

What happened?

What happened?

What happened?

What Happened

Autism & PDD: Abstract Concepts, Level 2   34

What happened?

What happened?

What happened?

What happened?

What happened?

What happened?

What happened?

What happened?

What happened?

What happened?

What happened?

What happened?

47

What happened?

What happened?

This section allows the child a novel way to answer questions logically. In responding to these questions, the child may draw from personal experiences or the experiences of others.

Directions

1. Photocopy each picture and fold up the bottom of each page to cover up the pictured response.

2. Have the child look at a picture. Read the question "What do you do when . . .?" Allow the child time to think about and formulate a response.

3. If the child gives an appropriate response, unfold the page to show the pictured response of the child's correct answer.

4. If the child has difficulty formulating a complete or specific response, unfold the page to provide a visual prompt while you provide a verbal model and repeat the question. The picture at the bottom of the page serves as a visual prompt by depicting the correct response.

Example

Stimulus (page 56)━━━━━━▶

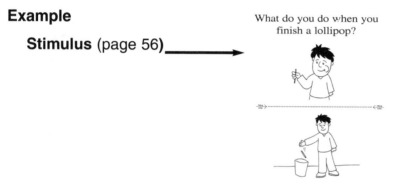

What do you do when you finish a lollipop?

Appropriate Responses

Beginner ⬇	Intermediate ⬇	Advanced ⬇
Single-Word Response	Multiple-Word Response	Complex Utterance
"Stick."	"Throw away stick."	"When you finish a lollipop, you throw away the stick."

Other Suggestions

-   Act out similar situations. Drop your crayon or listen to the phone ring. Pretend not to know what to do. Ask the child, "What do I do when . . . ?"

-   Reverse the form of your questions. For example, ask the child, "When do I give a present?" or "When do you put sunglasses on?"

What do you do when your soda is too warm?

Fold up ➤ to line— ◄ Fold up to line

What do you do when the cookie sheet is too hot to touch?

What do you do when you get in a car?

Fold up to line  Fold up to line

What do you do when you want to use your sister's CD player?

What do you do when you are writing with a pencil and you make a mistake?

Fold up to line   Fold up to line

What do you do when you finish a lollipop?

Fold up to line ▷ - ◁ Fold up to line

What do you do when the microwave beeps?

Fold up to line   Fold up to line

What do you do when the fire alarm sounds at school?

Fold up to line — Fold up to line

What do you do when your pencil point breaks?

Fold up to line

Fold up to line

What do you do when someone takes your picture?

Fold up
to line

Fold up
to line

What do you do when you have a toothache?

Fold up to line > - < Fold up to line

What do you do when you finish playing a game?

What do you do at the register of a store?

What do you do when you bring food home from the grocery store?

What do you do when you see a friend?

What do you do when you see smoke coming from a house?

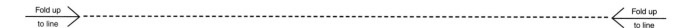
Fold up to line — Fold up to line

What do you do when you see someone stealing something?

Fold up to line

Fold up to line

What do you do when you go to the library?

What do you do when you leave home?

Fold up > to line Fold up < to line

What do you do when you get a mosquito bite?

Fold up
to line

Fold up
to line

What do you do when your plant is droopy?

Fold up to line --- Fold up to line

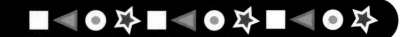
"Why . . . ?" is one of the more difficult *Wh* questions and is generally one of the last question types children comprehend. Review the child's ability to answer *who, what,* and *where* questions prior to beginning this section.

Directions

1. Photocopy each picture and fold up the bottom of each page to cover up the pictured response.

2. Have the child look at the picture. Read the question at the top of the page and allow the child time to think and give a correct response. Ask the child to color in or draw the object/action that shows the answer to the question. (If the child is unable to color independently, use hand-over-hand guidance to help him or her color.) For example, to answer *Why do people use paper plates?,* the child could draw a wastebasket.

3. If the child gives an appropriate response, unfold the page to show the pictured response as a reinforcement of the child's correct answer.

4. If the child has difficulty formulating a complete or specific response, unfold the page to provide a visual prompt while you provide a verbal model and repeat the question.

Example

Stimulus (page 82) ⟶

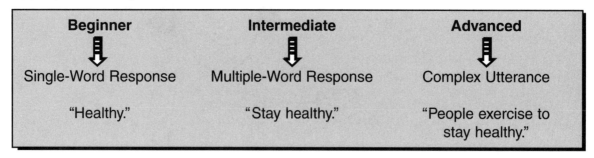

Why do people exercise?

Appropriate Responses

Beginner	**Intermediate**	**Advanced**
⬇	⬇	⬇
Single-Word Response	Multiple-Word Response	Complex Utterance
"Healthy."	"Stay healthy."	"People exercise to stay healthy."

Other Suggestions

• Act out situations in symbolic play in which you pretend to be disappointed, proud, sad, etc. Have the child tell why you are laughing, crying, etc. For example, pretend to stub your toe and have the child tell why you are crying.

• To try more advanced *why* questions, tell a short story or read a short book and have the child answer simple *why* questions about the story.

Why do people have cell phones?

Why do some coats have hoods?

Why do people use paper plates?

Fold up
to line

Fold up
to line

Why do people put on pajamas before they go to sleep?

Why do some boats have oars?

Fold up to line → ← Fold up to line

Why do some bicycles have a basket?

Fold up to line > - < Fold up to line

Why do watering cans have holes?

Fold up to line ⟩ - ⟨ Fold up to line

Why do some people drink coffee in the morning?

Why do some women wear makeup?

Fold up to line > --- < Fold up to line

Why do people exercise?

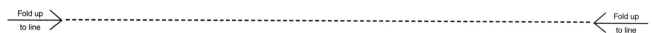

Fold up to line > < Fold up to line

Why do some men shave their faces?

Fold up to line   Fold up to line

Why do cars have windshield wipers?

Fold up
to line

Fold up
to line
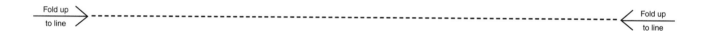

Why do people have mailboxes?

Fold up to line ⟩ — ⟨ Fold up to line

Why do houses have windows?

Why do people take medicine?

Fold up > to line

Fold up < to line

Why do some people wear glasses?

Why do we brush our teeth?

Fold up to line   Fold up to line

Why do people lock their doors?

Fold up > to line

< Fold up to line

Why do kids go to school?

Fold up to line →   ← Fold up to line

Why do people go to work?

Fold up to line ‹- -› Fold up to line

Why do people say "please" and "thank you"?

Why do you look before you cross the street?

Why do you wear a helmet when you ride your bike?

Fold up
to line ————————————————————————————————————— Fold up
to line

Why do you wear a seat belt in a car?

Why don't you eat cereal with a fork?

Why don't you wear shoes to bed?

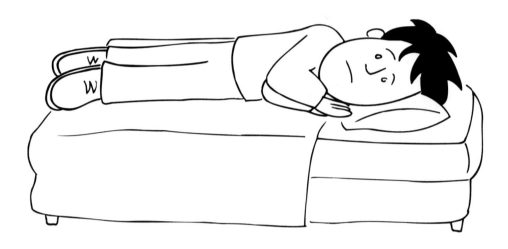

Fold up to line

Fold up to line

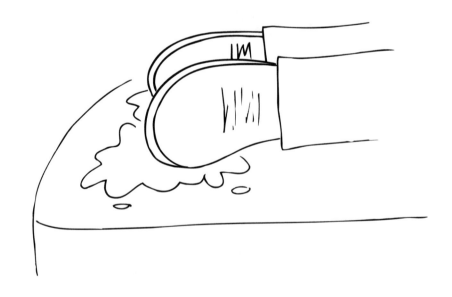

Why don't you let a dog run loose?

Fold up → to line   ← Fold up to line

Why don't you pile your clothes on the floor?

Fold up to line

Fold up to line

Why don't fish have legs?

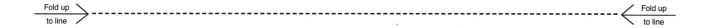

Fold up to line →   ← Fold up to line

Why don't you cut with a spoon?

Fold up
to line

Fold up
to line

Why don't you pet an alligator?

Fold up to line — Fold up to line

Why don't you swim outside in the winter?

Why don't you eat candy for breakfast?

Fold up to line > — < Fold up to line

Why do people mow their lawns?

This section teaches the child to make and express predictions. Given specific pieces of information, the child predicts what someone will do. Before beginning this section, the child needs to understand the concept of drawing conclusions and to use the modal *going to* (or *gonna*) to express personal intentions.

Directions

1. Photocopy each picture and fold up the bottom of each page to cover up the pictured response.

2. Have the child look at a picture. Read the statement and question aloud. Allow the child time to think about and formulate a response.

3. If the child gives an appropriate response, unfold the page to show the pictured response of the child's correct answer.

4. When appropriate, let the child color the picture as a reinforcer. If the child is unable to respond appropriately, unfold the page. Provide a model of the correct response and repeat the question. In this case, the second picture on the page serves as a visual prompt.

Example

Nicholas has a leash.
What is he going to do?

Stimulus (page 125)

Appropriate Responses

Beginner	Intermediate	Advanced
⬇	⬇	⬇
Single-Word Response	Multiple-Word Response	Complex Utterance
"Walk."	"Walk dog."	"He is going to walk his dog."

Other Suggestions

- Show the child one or two items and ask the child to guess what you are going to do with them.

- In a naturalistic context, catch the child with items before she uses them (e.g., a toothbrush, crayon, or ball). Ask, "What are you going to do?" Provide verbal models, if needed, and repeat.

These kids are at home and all the lights went out.
What are they going to do?

Fold up to line

Fold up to line

Madison has a picture, a nail, and a hammer.
What is she going to do?

Austin has a telephone book with a page of pizza restaurants. What is he going to do?

Jasmine has scissors and a newspaper.
What is she going to do?

Fold up to line >

< Fold up to line

Josh has a CD and a portable CD player.
What is he going to do?

Fold up to line

Fold up to line

Abby has books in her backpack and a lunch box.
What is she going to do?

Fold up to line >  < Fold up to line

These boys have a tent and sleeping bags.
What are they going to do?

Jason has wood polish and a cloth.
What is he going to do?

Fold up to line > - < Fold up to line

Aaron has a ticket and he has packed his suitcase.
What is he going to do?

Fold up to line ----------------------------------- Fold up to line

Mr. Ravelli has a map and an address on a card.
What is he going to do?

Noah has a pile of snowballs. He is hiding from his brother.
What is he going to do?

John has a tub, a hose, and dog shampoo.
What is he going to do?

Fold up to line

Fold up to line

Olivia brought paper plates, cups, burgers, hot dogs, and soda to the park. What is she going to do?

Fold up to line

Fold up to line

Mrs. Stone has a list of foods and her purse.
What is she going to do?

These kids are holding tickets. They are wearing baseball hats and jerseys. What are they going to do?

Fold up to line - Fold up to line

Hannah has a rake and a big black bag.
What is she going to do?

Fold up
to line — Fold up
to line

Mr. Gibbs is looking in the phone book. His water pipe is leaking. What is he going to do?

Fold up to line ⟩ - ⟨ Fold up to line

Nicholas has a leash.
What is he going to do?

Fold up to line > < Fold up to line

These people have matches, some logs, and marshmallows.
What are they going to do?

Fold up to line ▷ --------------------------------- ◁ Fold up to line

Grace has a fish in a bag and an empty bowl.
What is she going to do?

Fold up
to line Fold up
to line

In this section, children are asked to demonstrate simple organizational skills, which are important prerequisites for such tasks as verbal sequencing and basic storytelling.

Directions

1. Photocopy each picture before presenting it to the child.

2. Have the child look at the picture. Read the question. Allow the child time to think and respond appropriately. Draw in the items named in the child's response. For example, in responding to the question *What do you need to cook pasta?*, draw (or have the child draw) a pot filled with water on the stove. Use the drawings as a reinforcer. When appropriate, allow the child to color the drawings, or use hand-over-hand guidance. If the child is unable to respond appropriately, provide a model of the correct response, draw in the named items and repeat the question. In this case, the drawings serve as a visual prompt.

Example

What do you need to cook pasta?

Stimulus (page 134) ⟶

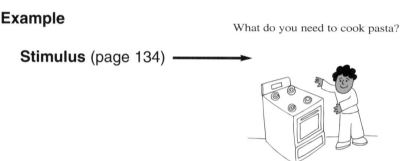

Appropriate Responses

Beginner	Intermediate	Advanced
⬇	⬇	⬇
Single-Word Response	Multiple-Word Response	Complex Utterance
"Pot."	"Pot of water."	"You need a pot full of water to cook pasta."

Other Suggestions

• Try other scenarios and have the child name up to three, four, or five items.

• Suggest activities to do with the child, such as coloring or baking. Have the child name the items needed before doing the activity you named.

What do you need to make pizza?

What do you need to get something off of the roof?

What do you need to have a party?

What do you need to take a picture?

What do you need to mail a letter?

What do you need to cook pasta?

What do you need to wrap a gift?

What do you need to form a band?

What do you need to have a lemonade stand?

What do you need to move a pile of dirt?

What do you need to wash a car?

What do you need to make a salad?

What do you need to build a fort in your house?

What do you need to make a jack-o'-lantern?

What do you need to make a birthday card?

What Do You Need

Autism & PDD: Abstract Concepts, Level 2   143

What do you need to start a campfire?

What does a barber need to give a haircut?

What does he need to get dressed for school?

By responding to questions in this section, children demonstrate beginning logic and problem-solving skills.

Directions

1. Photocopy each picture and fold up the bottom of each page to cover up the pictured response.

2. Have the child look at the picture. Read the question at the top of the page. Allow the child time to think about the answer and respond.

3. If the child gives an appropriate response, unfold the page to show the pictured response of the child's correct answer.

4. If the child has difficulty formulating a complete or specific response, unfold the page to provide a visual prompt while you provide a verbal model and repeat the question. The picture at the bottom of the page serves as a visual prompt by depicting the correct response.

Example

Stimulus (page 157) ⟶

Ben stepped in a mud puddle.
What should he do?

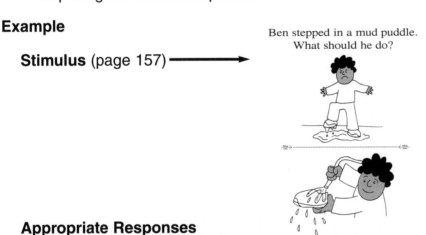

Appropriate Responses

Beginner	Intermediate	Advanced
⬇	⬇	⬇
Single-Word Response	Multiple-Word Response	Complex Utterance
"Shoe."	"Clean shoe."	"He should clean his shoe."

Other Suggestions

- Act out *What should* situations in play. Spill something "accidentally." Then have the child explain what you should do.

- Act out novel situations and play "dumb," prompting the child to initiate a solution to the problem or situation.

Andrew is in a restaurant. He wants more soda.
What should he do?

Fold up to line - Fold up to line

Emily is lost in a mall.
What should she do?

Fold up to line > - < Fold up to line

Mr. Clark's car broke down on the road.
What should he do?

Fold up to line ▷ -- ◁ Fold up to line

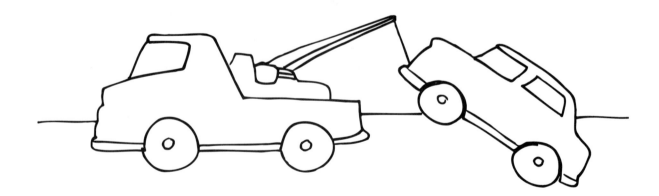

Jesse's friend has no lunch.
What should Jesse do?

Fold up > to line   < Fold up to line

Logan's hair is too long.
What should he do?

Nathaniel can't swim, but he wants to go in the pool.
What should he do?

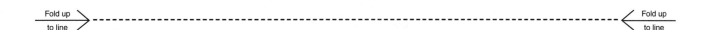

Fold up to line ┄┄┄┄┄┄┄┄┄┄┄┄┄┄┄┄┄┄┄┄┄┄┄┄┄┄┄┄┄┄ Fold up to line

Sam bought a shirt, but it's too small.
What should he do?

Gabriel wants to play outside, but it's raining. What should he do?

Kayla knows the answer to the teacher's question.
What should she do?

Fold up to line > — < Fold up to line

Ben stepped in a mud puddle.
What should he do?

There are many leaves on the ground.
What should Emma do?

Mario has a lot of money at home.
What should she do?

- -

Spencer can't carry his bag. It's too heavy.
What should he do?

- -

Anna's dog was injured.
What should she do?

Mrs. Lee's light bulb burned out.
What should she do?

Fold up to line ⟩ - ⟨ Fold up to line

Evan needs to cross a busy street.
What should he do?

Fold up
to line

Fold up
to line

Mr. Carson needs to make a cake. He doesn't have the ingredients.
What should he do?

Luke's ball went in the neighbor's yard.
What should he do?

Danielle's soup is too hot.
What should she do?

Fold up to line - Fold up to line

Problem-solving skills are important in both cognitive and language development. By answering *What if...?* questions, children are able to talk about and hypothesize about events they have not experienced themselves.

Directions

1. Photocopy each picture and fold up the bottom of each page to cover up the pictured response.

2. Have the child look at the picture. Read the question and allow the child time to think about the answer and respond.

3. If the child gives an appropriate response, unfold the page to show the pictured response of the child's correct answer.

4. If the child has difficulty formulating a complete or specific response, unfold the page to provide a visual prompt while you provide a verbal model and repeat the question. The picture at the bottom of the page serves as a visual prompt by depicting the correct response.

Example

What happens if you erase too hard?

Stimulus (page 171) ————————▶

Appropriate Responses

Beginner ⬇	Intermediate ⬇	Advanced ⬇
Single-Word Response	Multiple-Word Response	Complex Utterance
"Rip."	"Rip paper."	"If you erase too hard, you will rip the paper."

Other Suggestions

- Demonstrate *What if* situations in play. Let go of a balloon or step on something slippery. Have the child hypothesize what is going to happen.

- Read a story to the child. Before turning the pages, have the child guess what is going to happen next.

What happens if you eat something that is too spicy?

Fold up to line ─ ─ ─ ─ ─ ─ ─ ─ ─ ─ ─ ─ ─ ─ ─ Fold up to line

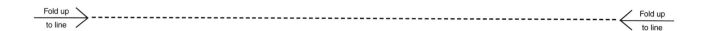

What happens if you leave milk on the counter too long?

Fold up to line

Fold up to line

What happens if you ride your bicycle over a nail?

What happens if you erase too hard?

Fold up to line > < Fold up to line

What happens if you miss the school bus?

Fold up to line   Fold up to line

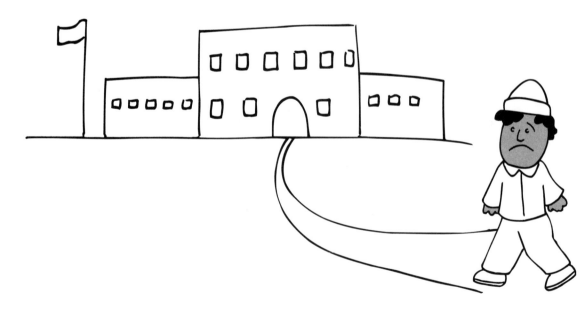

What happens if you spin around too much?

Fold up to line

Fold up to line

What If

Autism & PDD: Abstract Concepts, Level 2

173

What happens if you stay up too late?

Fold up to line   Fold up to line

What happens if you forget your house key and no one is home?

Fold up to line

Fold up to line

What happens if your car runs out of gas?

Fold up to line ⟩ - ⟨ Fold up to line

What happens if you step in poison ivy?

Fold up to line ⟩ - ⟨ Fold up to line

What happens if you walk in front of someone on a swing?

What happens if you sit on a bench that was just painted?

What happens if you leave your papers out on a windy day?

Fold up to line

Fold up to line

What happens if you step on gum?

Fold up to line >   < Fold up to line

What If

Autism & PDD: Abstract Concepts, Level 2　　　　181

What happens if you throw water on fire?

What happens if you throw a burning match on wood?

What happens if you leave a window open when it's raining?

Fold up > to line - < Fold up to line

What happens if you leave a pot boiling on the stove?

Fold up to line > ------------------------------- < Fold up to line

What happens if you tickle a baby?

Fold up > to line

< Fold up to line

What happens if you make bees angry?

Fold up to line

Fold up to line

What happens if you don't eat your breakfast?

Fold up to line

Fold up to line

What happens if you don't put the top on a blender?

Fold up to line   Fold up to line

What happens if you don't look where you are going?

Describing Feelings

Page

8   He feels proud.
9   He feels frustrated.
10 She feels proud.
11 He feels frustrated.
12 He feels disappointed.
13 He feels nervous.
14 She feels frustrated.
15 He feels embarrassed.
16 He feels embarrassed.
17 He feels frustrated.
18 He feels embarrassed.
19 She feels surprised.
20 He feels nervous.
21 He feels surprised.

What Happened

Page

23 The girl lost her tooth and got money from the tooth fairy.
24 The boy held his arms up on the roller coaster.
25 The man's hat flew off his head.
26 The boy made a snowman with three eyes, three arms, and two noses.
27 The dog ate the flowers.
28 Toilet paper stuck to her shoe.
29 The horse stood up and the boy fell off.
30 The girl put on her mom's makeup.
31 The girl was camping and it started to rain.
32 The boys played in the dirt with their suits on.
33 The lights went out in a storm.
34 The boy forgot to let go of the bowling ball.
35 The baseball team won a trophy.
36 It snowed so much that it covered the car.
37 The boy got a badge.
38 The fish pulled the fishing line.
39 The girl put ketchup on her pie.

40 The man drove into the stop sign.
41 The boy broke his arm and the girl signed his cast.
42 The girl broke the lamp and got in trouble.
43 The boy caught his friend instead of a butterfly.
44 A bee stung the boy.
45 The girl's dad took off her training wheels.
46 The boy's boat sank.
47 The boy buried his dad in the sand.
48 The boy was flying a kite and the string broke.
49 The boys saw a shooting star in the sky.

What Do You Do When

Page

51 When your soda is too warm, you put ice in it.
52 When the cookie sheet is too hot to touch, you use potholders.
53 When you get in a car, you put on your seat belt.
54 When you want to use your sister's CD player, you ask her.
55 When you are writing with a pencil and you make a mistake, you erase it.
56 When you finish a lollipop, you throw away the stick.
57 When the microwave beeps, you take the food out.
58 When the fire alarm sounds at school, you go outside.
59 When your pencil point breaks, you sharpen it.
60 When someone takes your picture, you smile.
61 When you have a toothache, you go to the dentist.
62 When you finish playing a game, you put it away.
63 When you are at the register, you pay for what you are buying.
64 When you bring food home from the grocery store, you put it away.
65 When you see a friend, you greet him.
66 When you see smoke coming from a house, you call the fire department.
67 When you see someone stealing, you call the police.
68 When you go to the library, you check out books.
69 When you leave home, you lock the door.
70 When you get a mosquito bite, you scratch it.
71 When your plant is droopy, you water it.

Why/Because

Page

73 People have cell phones so they can call people.
74 Some coats have hoods to keep your head warm/dry.
75 People use paper plates so they can throw them away.
76 People put pajamas on before they go to sleep so they can be comfortable.
77 Some boats have oars so you can row them.
78 Some bicycles have baskets so you can carry things in them.
79 Watering cans have holes so the water can come out.
80 Some people drink coffee in the morning so they can wake up.
81 Some women wear makeup to look nice.
82 People exercise to stay healthy.
83 Some men shave their faces so they don't grow beards.
84 Cars have windshield wipers so you can see when it rains.
85 People have mailboxes so they can get mail.
86 Houses have windows so you can see outside.
87 People take medicine so they can feel better.
88 Some people wear glasses so they can see better.
89 We brush our teeth so we don't get cavities.
90 People lock their doors so no one else can get inside.
91 Kids go to school so they can learn.
92 People go to work so they can earn money.
93 People say "please" and "thank you" because it's polite.
94 You look before you cross the street so you don't get hit by a car.
95 You wear a helmet when you ride your bike to protect your head.
96 You wear a seat belt in a car to keep you safe.
97 You don't eat cereal with a fork because the milk will spill through.
98 You don't wear shoes to bed because it would get the bed dirty.
99 You don't let a dog run loose because it can get lost.
100 You don't pile your clothes on the floor because then you have nothing to wear.
101 Fish don't have legs because they don't walk, they swim.
102 You don't cut with a spoon because it's not sharp.
103 You don't pet an alligator because it will bite you.
104 You don't swim outside in the winter because it's too cold.
105 You don't eat candy for breakfast because it's not good for you.
106 People mow their lawns so the grass doesn't grow too high.

Going To

Page

108 They are going to get a flashlight.
109 She is going to hang the picture.
110 He is going to order a pizza.
111 She is going to cut something out of the paper.
112 He is going to listen to music.
113 She is going to go to school.
114 They are going to sleep outside.
115 He is going to polish the table.
116 He is going to take a trip.
117 He is going to look for a house.
118 He is going to throw a snowball.
119 He is going to wash his dog.
120 She is going to have a picnic.
121 She is going to buy groceries.
122 They are going to a baseball game.
123 She is going to rake leaves.
124 He is going to call a plumber.
125 He is going to walk his dog.
126 They are going to roast some marshmallows.
127 She is going to put the fish in the bowl.

What Do You Need

Page

129 You need dough, sauce, and cheese to make pizza.
130 You need a ladder to get something off of the roof.
131 You need food, drinks, and people to have a party.
132 You need a camera and film to take a picture.
133 You need an envelope and a stamp to mail a letter.
134 You need a pot full of water to cook pasta.
135 You need wrapping paper, scissors, and tape to wrap a gift.
136 You need instruments (guitar, drums, keyboard) to form a band.
137 You need cups, a pitcher of lemonade, and a sign to have a lemonade stand.
138 You need a shovel and a wheelbarrow to move a pile of dirt.
139 You need soap, a sponge, and a bucket of water to wash a car.

140 You need lettuce, tomatoes, cucumbers, and dressing to make a salad.
141 You need cushions, pillows, and blankets to build a fort in your house.
142 You need a pumpkin, a knife, and a candle to make a jack-o'-lantern.
143 You need paper and crayons to make a birthday card.
144 You need wood and matches to start a campfire.
145 He needs scissors and a comb to give a haircut.
146 He needs pants, a shirt, and shoes to get dressed for school.

What Should

Page

148 He should ask the waiter for more soda.
149 She should find a guard.
150 He should call a tow truck.
151 He should share his lunch with his friend.
152 He should get a haircut.
153 He should wear a life preserver/swimmies.
154 He should take it back to the store.
155 He should play inside.
156 She should raise her hand.
157 He should clean his shoe.
158 She should rake the leaves.
159 He should put the money in the bank.
160 He should get a cart with wheels.
161 She should take the dog to a veterinarian.
162 She should put in a new light bulb.
163 He should wait for the crossing guard.
164 He should buy the ingredients at the grocery store.
165 He should ask the neighbor to get the ball.
166 She should blow on the soup.

What If

Page

168 If you eat something that is too spicy, you will burn your tongue.
169 If you leave milk on the counter too long, it will spoil.
170 If you ride your bicycle over a nail, you will get a flat tire.
171 If you erase too hard, you will rip the paper.

172 If you miss the school bus, you will be late for school.
173 If you spin around too much, you will get dizzy.
174 If you stay up too late, you will be tired the next day.
175 If you forget your house key and no one is home, you will be locked out of your house.
176 If your car runs out of gas, your car won't go.
177 If you step in poison ivy, you will get an itchy rash.
178 If you walk in front of someone on a swing, you will get hit.
179 If you sit on a bench that was just painted, you will get paint on your clothes.
180 If you leave your papers out on a windy day, the wind will blow them away.
181 If you step on gum, your shoe will stick to the floor.
182 If you throw water on a fire, it will go out.
183 If you throw a burning match on wood, you will start a fire.
184 If you leave a window open when it's raining, your floor will get wet.
185 If you leave a pot boiling on the stove, it will bubble over.
186 If you tickle a baby, the baby will laugh.
187 If you make bees angry, they will sting you.
188 If you don't eat your breakfast, you will get hungry.
189 If you don't put the top on a blender, the food will splatter.
190 If you don't look where you are going, you will bump into something.

21-02-987654321

Answer Key

Autism & PDD: Abstract Concepts, Level 2   196